66 Year-Round CRAFTS for Preschoolers

Carolyn Strom Collins and Christina Wyss Eriksson

Prince Paperbacks/New York

Published by Crown Publishers, Inc., 201 East 50th Street, New York, New York 10022.
Member of the Crown Publishing Group.

Random House, Inc. New York, Toronto, London, Sydney, Auckland

Prince Paperbacks and colophon are trademarks of Crown Publishers, Inc.

Manufactured in the U.S.A.

Design and Illustration by Jennifer Harper

Library of Congress Cataloging-in-Publication Data
Collins, Carolyn Strom.
66 year-round crafts for preschoolers / by Carolyn Strom Collins and Christina Wyss Eriksson.
p.   cm.
1. Handicraft. 2. Holiday decorations. I. Eriksson, Christina Wyss. II. Title.
TT157.C545 1994
745.594'1—dc20

ISBN 0-517-88066-0
10 9 8 7 6 5 4 3 2 1

First Edition

For Claire and Evan

Contents

Acknowledgments

We acknowledge with thanks the able assistants of our agent Jeanne Hanson
and of our editors at Crown, Irene Prokop and Sharon Squibb,
and the designer of this book, Jennifer Harper.

Introduction

The crafts in this book have been developed especially with preschoolers (ages three and up) in mind. They are made with readily available, inexpensive materials, and most can be completed in one session. A few, such as the Mini-Greenhouse and Potpourri, are begun in one session and develop over several days.

The projects were selected not only to entertain the children but also to give them a sense of accomplishment, to develop their interest in and awareness of the different seasons, and to encourage their participation in the many holidays throughout the year.

66 Year-Round CRAFTS for Preschoolers

New Year's Day

Time Capsule

Start the new year with memories of the old one by making your own "time capsule" containing mementos of the past year. The time capsule can be hidden away and opened next New Year's Day, which is a nice tradition.

Materials Needed:

Potato chip canister (or similar container) with lid

Adhesive-backed paper, stickers, or construction paper and glue

Scissors

Small items to place in canister

(such as a school photo of child, family photos, samples of child's artwork, small toy, memento(s) of a vacation trip, pencil outline of child's hand, notes on child's height and weight, names of child's teacher and friends, etc.)

Adult's Preparation: Collect materials needed. Help child decorate canister. Help child select items to place in canister. Help child write her name and the date.

Child's Activity: Decorate canister as desired with adhesive-backed paper, stickers, or construction paper. Place items such as a photograph of yourself, an outline of your

hand, a small toy, some of your own artwork, something you may have brought back from a trip (such as a seashell or some pebbles or a postcard), and anything else you want in your own "time capsule." Include a piece of paper with your name and the date on it. Put the lid on and hide the time capsule away in a drawer or closet until next New Year's Day, when you can open it up and look at the contents again.

Confetti Pretzels

Celebrate the new year with a fun and festive snack.

Materials Needed:

Large bag miniature pretzels

16-ounce package white "chocolate" candy coating

Candy "confetti" dots

Bowl and mixing spoon

Waxed paper

Adult's Preparation: Assemble materials. Melt white candy coating according to package directions. To keep coating soft enough to dip into, place the bowl in a pan of very warm water.

Child's Activity: Dip each pretzel in the white candy coating. Let excess run off, then place pretzels on waxed paper. Sprinkle the pretzels with candy confetti while they're still wet, then let the decorated pretzels dry.

Piñata

The piñata game is a holiday tradition in Mexico. Each child, in turn, is blindfolded and given a stick to swing at the piñata, which hangs overhead. When the piñata breaks, all the children scramble to pick up the candies and small toys that fall to the floor.

Materials Needed:

Brown paper bag, lunch-size (for individual piñatas)
   or grocery-size (for group piñata)
Crepe paper streamers in various bright colors,
   any length
Glue
Assorted wrapped candies and toys to fill piñata
   one-third to one-half full
Ribbon or string, about 36 inches long

Adult's Preparation: Assemble materials. Fringe crepe paper streamers by cutting small strips to within about ½ inch from top edge. Hang piñata.

Child's Activity: Glue top edge of streamer to paper bag; continue until it is covered in fringed paper.

Fill bag one-third to one-half full of candy and small toys. Gather the top of the bag closed and tie with ribbon or string. Then, with the long ends of the ribbon or string, tie the piñata just overhead. Now you are ready to start the piñata game.

Chinese New Year

Dragon Mask

A fierce dragon is part of this ancient celebration. Make your own dragon mask and join in the fun.

Materials Needed:

Brown paper bag with square bottom, medium (about 8 inches wide)

Construction paper, 1 or 2 sheets each of several colors

Glue

Scissors

Adult's Preparation: Assemble materials. Help child cut out eyes, mouth, teeth, scales, etc., for his mask. Cut eyeholes in the paper bag to fit child.

Child's Activity: Cut out dragon eyes, mouth, teeth, scales, and other features from construction paper. Glue onto the paper bag around the eyeholes. Wear the dragon mask and practice your fiercest dragon roar.

Chinese Noodle Cookies

Another way to celebrate Chinese New Year is with these treats made from Chinese noodles.

Materials Needed:

1 cup (6-ounce package) chocolate chips
1 cup (6-ounce package) butterscotch chips
2 cups (12-ounce package) crunchy Chinese
    noodles
1 cup roasted peanuts (optional)
Large mixing bowl
Spoons for mixing and dropping cookies
Waxed paper

Adult's Preparation: Assemble materials. Melt butterscotch and chocolate chips over hot water or in microwave oven. Help child mix and spoon out cookies.

Child's Activity: Carefully stir Chinese noodles and peanuts into the chocolate and butterscotch mixture until they are coated. Spoon out in small mounds onto waxed paper and let cool. Enjoy!

Groundhog Day

Groundhog Puppet

It is said that the groundhog wakes up from his winter's nap on February 2 and comes out of his hole to see if it is time for spring. If he doesn't see his shadow, he believes spring is on the way, and he will stay awake. But if he does see his shadow, he hurries back down to sleep for another six weeks of winter.

Materials Needed:

Construction paper, 1 sheet each of light brown and green

Scissors

Crayons

Popsicle or craft stick

Glue

Adult's Preparation: Assemble materials. Trace groundhog shape onto construction paper. Help child cut out groundhog and attach it to stick; help cut slit in paper for groundhog puppet to slide in and out.

Child's Activity: Fold a sheet of construction paper in half and cut out a groundhog shape. On one of the shapes, draw a groundhog face with crayons. Glue the two shapes together along with a Popsicle or craft stick at the bottom for a handle.

In the middle of another sheet of construction paper, cut a slit just a little wider than the groundhog puppet. Put the puppet into the slit from the back of the paper. Make the groundhog go in and out of his "hole" to see his shadow.

Maybe you can make up a little play or poem or song about your groundhog puppet.

Silly Shadows

While the groundhog is looking for his shadow, children can have fun with their own shadows.

Materials Needed:

Large piece of plain paper
   (brown wrapping paper, newsprint, etc.)
Masking tape
Bright light
Crayons and/or paint (optional)
Yarn (optional)
Glue (optional)

Adult's Preparation: Assemble materials. Tape large piece of paper to wall. Position light so that child's shadow will appear on the paper. Trace outline of child onto paper.

Child's Activity: Stand between the light and the piece of paper. Arrange your arms, legs, hands, feet, and head in a silly position. Have someone trace all around your shadow. Color or paint in your face and clothes. Cut around the lines for a silhouette shape. Glue on pieces of yarn for hair, if desired. Hang silhouette up for a decoration.

Peanut Butter Play Dough

Groundhogs love peanut butter, so Groundhog Day is the perfect time to make some of this edible peanut butter play dough.

Materials Needed:
2 cups (16-ounce jar) smooth peanut butter
1 cup (8 ounces) honey
2 cups powdered milk
Large mixing bowl
Wooden spoon, rubber spatula
Apron
Clean hands!

Adult's Preparation: Assemble materials. Help child measure ingredients, pointing out the measurement marks on the cups. Help child mix the dough.

Child's Activity: Wash your hands! Taste a little of the peanut butter, honey, and powdered milk. With the wooden spoon, mix the peanut butter and honey in the large bowl. Taste that, too! Now add the powdered milk

and stir that in until everything is mixed well. You may have to use your hands to finish the mixing. Taste the play dough—can you taste the three different ingredients in it or does it now have a new taste all its own?

Break off pieces to make shapes—worms, pretzels, cups with handles, flowers, teddy bears, maybe even a groundhog! You can eat them, let them dry out, or put them back in the bowl and smoosh them all up to make more shapes!

Store any leftover play dough in the refrigerator in a plastic bag; bring to room temperature to play with again.

St. Valentine's Day

Woven Heart Ornament or Wall Hanging

Make a small heart for a tree ornament or a large one for a wall hanging. The heart motif can be used as a Valentine's Day or Christmas decoration.

Materials Needed:

Construction paper, 2 colors, 2 sheets each
    (red/white, pink/white, red/pink, red/green, etc.)
Scissors
Glue
Ribbon or string, 24 inches long

Adult's Preparation: Assemble materials. Cut out basic pattern from both colors of construction paper or draw them on paper

for child to cut out. Patterns can be any size, from about 5 inches high for a smaller heart to 11 inches high for a large heart; the two parts should be the same size, however. Show child how to weave strips together.

Child's Activity: Cut each pattern piece halfway up into 4 equal strips. Overlap the two pattern pieces to form a heart shape, and weave the strips together (see illustration). Glue in several places to hold them together. Punch a small hole in the top and thread a piece of ribbon or string through to make a hanging loop.

Hand-Heart Card
A Charming keepsake for Valentine's Day!

Materials Needed:
Construction paper, pink and red (1 sheet of pink and piece of red for each card)
Pencil
Scissors
Glue
Crayons

Adult's Preparation: Assemble materials. Make a heart "stencil" for child to trace. Help child write message and name.

Child's Activity: Fold sheet of pink construction paper in half like a book (8½ inches × 5½ inches). Place your left hand on top of the

folded paper with your little finger and wrist along the folded edge. Trace around your fingers and hand with a pencil, starting at the top of your little finger all the way around to the bottom of your thumb. Cut around your handprint through both layers of paper, except for the left folded side.

Cut out a heart (about 2 inches high) from the red construction paper and glue it inside the card as shown in the illustration. Write a Valentine's Day message and your name on the inside of the card.

President's Day

General Washington's Hat

Before George Washington became our first president, he was a general in the army. Here is how to make a hat like the one he wore when he was leading the fight for American independence.

Materials Needed:

Newspaper or other paper, 14 inches × 22 inches

Tape

Adult's Preparation: Assemble materials. Help child with folding.

Child's Activity: Fold paper in half to measure 14 inches × 11 inches. Place paper on table with fold away from you. Grasp the top two corners of the folded edge and bring them down toward the center until they meet in the middle. The folds should make a triangle shape (see illustration). Crease the

edges so they will lie flat. Fold the bottom margins up on the front and back of the hat to make a "cuff." Tape the bottom corners for extra strength.

Abraham Lincoln's Log Cabin

Abraham Lincoln was our sixteenth president. He grew up in a log cabin, which is a house made of trees that have been cut and stacked to fit together.

Materials Needed:

Construction paper, 1 sheet of light blue
Small sticks and twigs, about 6 inches long
Glue
Crayons

Adult's Preparation: Assemble materials. Help child draw outline of cabin and glue sticks onto paper. Tell child about Abraham Lincoln while working on the picture.

Child's Activity: Draw an outline of a cabin on the construction paper. Draw a door and a window or two. Glue sticks and twigs onto the paper in rows to look like stacked up logs. Break the sticks to fit into the outline. Leave spaces for the door and windows. Draw on extra features like a chimney, smoke, grass, and trees if you like.

St. Patrick's Day

Dancing Leprechaun Yarn Doll

This yarn doll loves to dance an Irish jig!

Materials Needed:
Heavy cardboard, 8 inches × 3 inches (for body)
Heavy cardboard, 6 inches × 3 inches (for arms)
Green yarn, about 20 yards
Scissors
Felt (optional)
Glue (optional)

Adult's Preparation: Assemble materials. Demonstrate winding and tying yarn and assembling doll. Cut a 1-yard piece of yarn from the skein for tying off arms and legs and for making the head and dancing string.

Child's Activity: Make the body of the doll by winding yarn around the longer piece of cardboard 24 times. Cut the end of the yarn and carefully slip the bundle off the cardboard. With a short piece of yarn, make a head for the doll by tying off the yarn bundle about 1 inch from the top.

For arms, wind yarn around the shorter piece of cardboard 24 times. Slip the yarn bundle off and tie with a short piece of yarn about ½ inch from each end for hands. Slide

arms into body just below the head. Tie body under the arms for a waist and to hold the arms on. If desired, tie the remainder of the body yarn into two parts for legs.

Tie a longer piece of yarn through some of the head loops so you can make the doll dance.

If you like, cut out some small circles of felt for eyes, mouth, and nose, and glue them on the head to make a face for your doll.

St. Patrick's Day Corsage

March 17 is St. Patrick's Day. Start this project the day before.

Materials Needed:

White carnation
Glass or bottle
Water
Green food coloring
Green florist's tape (optional)
Green ribbon
Safety pin

Adult's Preparation: Assemble materials. Help wrap tape around stem. Pin flower to child's shirt.

Child's Activity: Fill the glass or bottle halfway with water. Add several drops of food coloring until water is bright green. Cut the stem of the carnation to about 4 inches. Put the carnation in the glass or bottle of green water, stem end first. Let stand overnight. The next day, you should have a green carnation!

Remove the flower from the water; pat dry. Cut the stem to about 2 inches. Wrap in florist's tape, if desired. Tie a green ribbon bow on the stem. Pin the flower to your shirt for St. Patrick's Day. Does this make you want to do an Irish jig?

First Day of Spring

Handprint Bluebirds

Bluebirds are one of America's favorite birds. Children can be encouraged to watch for them, and other birds, in the spring.

Materials Needed:

White paper

Blue tempera paint

Orange construction paper, small piece

Scissors

Black pen or crayon

Glue

Pie tin

Apron or paint shirt

Adult's Preparation: Cover the worktable with newspapers. Pour a few tablespoons of blue tempera paint (medium consistency) into the pie tin. Show child how to press his hands into the paint and onto the paper to form a bird shape (see illustration). Help draw bird legs and glue on beak.

Child's Activity: Press hands, palms down, into blue paint. Make a print of both hands side by side on white paper, thumbs together, fingers apart. Wash hands. Cut a small triangle from orange construction paper and glue to the "thumbs" on your painting. This is the bluebird's beak. Draw eyes and legs on the bluebird with a black pen or crayon. Draw some trees in the background, too, or any scene you like behind the bluebird.

Jack-and-the-Beanstalk Plant Tower

Springtime is planting time. After hearing the story of "Jack and the Beanstalk," it will be fun for a child to plant her own beanstalk to grow inside a "castle tower."

Materials Needed:
Empty round oatmeal box or quart-size milk carton
Scissors or utility knife
   (for adult to use in preparation)
Styrofoam cup
Potting soil
Bean seeds
Water
Plastic drinking straw
2 twist ties
Construction paper
Glue
Crayons

Adult's Preparation: Assemble materials. Cover work area with newspapers. Cut a 2-inch "door" and a few 1-inch "windows" in

the box or carton for peepholes.

Child's Activity: With construction paper, glue, and crayons, decorate the box or carton to look like a castle tower. Scoop potting soil into the cup and plant 1 or 2 bean seeds about ½ inch deep; cover with a little more soil. Moisten with water. Place the cup inside the "tower." Stick the drinking straw into the cup—it will be a handy stake for the growing bean vine. (Use the twist ties to hold the vine to the "stake.") Keep the soil moist but not too wet. Set the bean tower in a warm, well-lit place. In a few days it will begin to grow, and before long, it will be growing up and out of the top of the tower! Then you can plant it in a bigger pot or outside in the garden. Be on the lookout for giants!

Breezy-Day Kite

Those windy days of March are blowing spring our way. Make a kite decoration to celebrate!

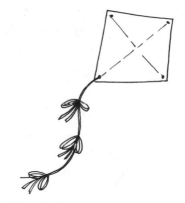

Materials Needed:

Construction paper, any color (8½ inches × 11 inches)

4 or 5 pieces of gift-wrap ribbon in various colors, each 6 inches long

Scissors

2 pieces of twine or yarn, each 16 inches long

2 reinforcing rings or tape (optional)

Adult's Preparation: Assemble materials. Draw pattern for kite on construction paper for child to follow (see illustration for pattern). Help child put kite together.

Child's Activity: Cut out diamond-shaped kite from construction paper. Tie pieces of ribbon to one length of twine or yarn about every 3 inches, starting about 6 inches from one end and ending at the very end of the twine; tie them in a tight knot so they will stay on! This is the kite's tail.

Cut or punch a small hole about ½ inch from the bottom point of the kite, slip the free end of the tail twine into it, and tie. Cut or punch another small hole about ½ inch from the top point of the kite and tie the other piece of twine on for carrying the kite. (It might be a good idea to reinforce these holes with stick-on reinforcing rings or tape to keep the kite from tearing.)

Passover

Herb Napkin Rings

Bitter herbs, such as parsley, are part of the Passover seder. These parsley napkin rings will give a special touch to your family meal.

Materials Needed:

Plain index cards, 3 inches × 5 inches
Scissors
Glue
Chopped dried parsley

Adult's Preparation: Assemble materials. Cover work area with newspaper. Cut index cards in half lengthwise to measure 1½ inches × 5 inches.

Child's Activity: Overlap ends of strips about ¼ inch and glue to form a ring. (You may have to put some tape on the inside to hold the ring closed.) Spread some glue about ¼–½ inch along the top and bottom rims of the ring. Roll the ring in the dried herbs until the edges are thickly covered. Set the napkin ring aside to dry.

When it is time to eat, put napkins into the napkin rings and place one beside each plate at the table.

Herb Place Cards

Continue the herb theme at the table with a place card for each person to match the napkin rings.

Materials Needed:

Plain index cards, 3 inches × 5 inches
(1 per person)
Glue
Chopped dried parsley
Crayon or pen

Adult's Preparation: Assemble materials. Cover work area with newspaper.

Child's Activity: Fold index card in half to measure 3 inches × 2½ inches. On one half, spread a border of glue about ¼–½ inch wide. While glue is wet, sprinkle dried parsley on the borders until they are thickly covered. Press the parsley down gently into the glue to make sure it sticks. Set the card aside to dry.

Before dinner, write each person's name on a card inside the parsley border, and bend the card at the fold so that it will stand up. Put the card at the place where the person is supposed to sit.

Easter

Easter Bunny Bag

Children will love carrying their own Easter Bunny bag on an egg hunt.

Materials Needed:

Shopping bag with square bottom and sturdy
    handles, small to medium
Construction paper, pink and white
    (2 sheets of each)
Scissors
Glue
Crayon (to draw whiskers)
Cotton balls
Cellophane "grass" or tissue paper

Adult's Preparation: Assemble materials. Cut out bunny ears, feet, eyes, and mouth from construction paper (see illustration) or draw patterns onto construction paper for child to cut out. Help child glue on face, ears, feet, and cotton tail.

Child's Activity: Paste feet on bottom of bag (they should stick out in front as shown). Paste ears, eyes, and mouth on front of bag. Draw on some whiskers. Glue a cotton ball onto the back of the bag for the bunny's "cotton tail." Put cellophane "grass" or tissue paper in the bottom of the bag to cushion the Easter eggs you will find on your egg hunt!

Easter Egg Holder

To display your colored Easter eggs, stand each one up in its very own holder.

Materials Needed:

Cardboard tube from paper towel or bathroom tissue
½-inch ribbon, pastel-colored (6 inches long)
Scissors
Glue

Adult's Preparation: Assemble materials. Cut cardboard tube into ½-inch rings. Show child how to wind ribbon around rings. Help child to cut and glue ribbon.

Child's Activity: Spread a thin layer of glue on the outside of the ring. Wrap the ribbon all the way around the ring. Glue the end of the ribbon down.

Make one ring for your favorite Easter egg or make enough rings for all the eggs you have colored. They would make a terrific centerpiece for Easter breakfast or dinner. Or make one ring for each member of your family and place them, complete with colored eggs, on a plate for Easter breakfast.

Easter Bunny Nibbling Cup

Children will enjoy discovering that bunnies like some of their own favorite foods, too!

Materials Needed:

Paper cup

Large lettuce leaves

Mixed raw vegetables, such as carrot and celery
    sticks, small radishes, broccoli and
    cauliflower florets

Raffia strip

Adult's Preparation: Assemble materials. Wash and dry lettuce and vegetables.

Child's Activity: Wrap 2 or 3 lettuce leaves around the cup. Let the curly edge of the lettuce stand up above the edge of the cup. Tie the lettuce leaves to the cup with a strip of raffia—wrap it around the cup twice for extra strength. Tear or trim off any lettuce that comes below the cup. Now fill the cup with veggies. Place outside for bunnies to find and nibble on. Maybe you should make an extra cup for yourself. Happy nibbling!

Arbor Day

A Family Tree

Arbor Day is a day when we pay special attention to trees and how much the earth needs them. Wouldn't this be a nice time to make a "family tree"?

Materials Needed:
Small flowerpot
Gravel or block of plastic foam
   (to anchor branch)
Small tree branch
Construction paper, any color
   (1 or 2 sheets)
Scissors
Crayons
Yarn, ribbon, or thread, about 1 yard
Family photos (optional)

Adult's Preparation: Assemble materials.

Child's Activity: Center the tree branch in the flowerpot and surround it with gravel to hold it upright. Or place a block of plastic foam in the flowerpot and anchor the branch in it. Cut 3–4-inch circles out of construction paper, one for each member of your family. Draw a face on each circle to look like a family member, or cut and glue on a photo.

Write the name underneath if you wish. Make a small hole in the top of the circle, put a piece of yarn, ribbon, or thread through it to make a hanging loop, tie the ends together, and hang the circles by the loop on the tree branch.

Milk Carton Birdhouse

Birds need trees even more than people do. Here is an easy birdhouse to hang in a tree. If you don't have a tree outside your window, you can mount the house on a flat surface.

Materials needed:

½-gallon milk carton, rinsed out
Wire, floral, 6 inches long
Twig or ¼-inch dowel, 6 inches long
Adhesive-backed vinyl-coated paper

Adult's Preparation: Punch small holes in the top ridge of the milk carton for wire loop. Cut a small slit in the lower front of the carton for the twig or ¼-inch dowel perch to fit into. Cut a 1–1½-inch hole for the door, about 2 inches from the bottom of the milk carton.

Child's Activity: Decorate the milk carton with adhesive-backed paper. Thread a piece of wire through the top holes and twist the ends together to make a loop. Put a twig or dowel into the slit under the door hole for the birds to perch on. Hang the birdhouse outside in a tree as a new home for birds or inside for a springtime decoration.

Tree Specimen Box

Learn more about a tree in your neighborhood by collecting a few items from it to display.

Materials Needed:

Shallow box, about 9 inches × 12 inches
Sheet of cotton batting, towel, or felt,
    about 9 inches × 12 inches
Slips of paper for making labels
Pencil or pen
Clear plastic wrap
Tape

Adult's Preparation: Assemble materials. Help child find and select items for the specimen box, reminding her not to damage the tree in the process (for example, the child should not strip any bark off the tree but should find a bit on the ground that has been shed naturally).

Child's Activity: Press the cotton batting, towel, or felt into the bottom of the box. Go outside and select a tree that you like and want to learn more about. See how many things you can collect from it to put in your specimen box: a leaf or two, some pieces of

bark (use only those pieces that you find on the ground—if you take bark from a tree, you might damage the tree), some twigs, flowers or seedpods, cones or acorns, etc.

Some other things you can add to your specimen box: Draw a picture of your tree or perhaps take a photograph of it. Give your tree a name and write it on a label for your specimen box.

Arrange the items on the cotton batting, towels, or felt in the specimen box. Make a label for each item.

Watch the tree in different seasons to see how it changes. For example, do the leaves change color in the fall? Do the leaves drop off after they change color? Do the branches bend and sway a lot when it is windy? Are there any birds or animals living in the tree? Can you find their nests? Are the flowers of the tree easy to find? Do they *look* like you think flowers should look or do they look different? Do the flowers turn into fruit or nuts or cones or seeds? What do they look like? Can you find tiny little "baby" trees like your big tree growing nearby? How long do you think it will take them to grow as tall as your big tree?

Earth Day

Mini-Greenhouse

Children can watch seeds sprout and grow in early spring, even when it is still too cold outside to plant.

Materials Needed:

Clear plastic hinged take-out food container, about 6 inches square

Potting soil

Grass seed or radish seeds

Spray bottle of water

Construction paper, old magazines, scissors (optional)

Adult's Preparation: Assemble materials. Cover work area with newspapers.

Child's Activity: Spread about ¾ inch of potting soil in the bottom of the plastic box. Sprinkle seeds liberally over the surface and gently press them into the soil. Moisten the entire surface with water from the spray bottle—not *too* much! Close the lid and place the box in a well-lit place (but not in direct sunlight). Lift the lid daily and keep the soil moist by spraying with water. Within several days, seeds should start to sprout, and in about 10 days, there should be a nice crop!

Decorate your new "lawn" with flowers and butterflies cut from construction paper, or from pictures in magazines, if you like.

Animal Cracker Pins

These are fun to wear anywhere but especially to the zoo or circus!

Materials Needed:

Animal crackers
  (be sure there are extras to nibble on!)
Varnish and small brush or clear nail polish
Adhesive-backed jewelry pins
Waxed paper

Adult's Preparation: Assemble materials. Cover work surface with newspapers. Put a piece of waxed paper at child's place to catch drips and to place cookie on between coats to dry. Supervise application of varnish or nail polish and help attach jewelry pins to finished cookie (peel off the paper backing and place in center of back of cookie).

Child's Activity: Paint back of cookie with 2 or 3 coats of varnish or nail polish (let dry on waxed paper between coats). Turn cookie over and paint front with 2 or 3 coats of varnish or nail polish. Paint the sides, too. When the cookie is dry, attach a jewelry pin to the back and pin the cookie to your shirt.

May Day

May Day Baskets

Hanging May baskets on neighbors' doors on the first day of May is a centuries-old tradition which you can start in your neighborhood. Surprise all your friends on May Day.

Materials Needed:

Paper plate (white or pastel color), 6–8 inches

White doily (same size or slightly larger than paper plate)

Ribbon, 16 inches long

Stapler and staples

Glue

Hole puncher

Spring flowers

Adult's Preparation: Assemble materials. Help child fold paper plate and staple it. Punch holes for ribbon and help knot ribbon ends.

Child's Activity: Fold paper plate and press into a flat cone shape (see illustration); staple to hold it closed. Cover with lacy paper doily and glue in place. Punch holes ¼ inch from top two corners and thread ribbon through to make a handle. Knot the ribbon ends securely. Fill basket with spring flowers. Hang the May basket on someone's doorknob for an extra-special May Day surprise!

Pretty Petals Plaque

This little plaque will be a nice reminder of the pretty flowers of May Day. You may want to make several for gifts.

Materials Needed:

Disposable pie tin or plate

Premixed plaster of paris

Fresh flowers, preferably sturdy flat ones such as yellow dandelions, daisies, or Queen Anne's lace; small fern leaves would also work

Pencil or skewer for making small holes in the plaque

Yarn, ribbon, or leather lacing, 8 inches long

Adult's Preparation: Assemble materials. Cover work surface with newspapers. Help child write his name and the date if he wants to add them.

Child's Activity: Scoop out enough plaster of paris to make a plaque about ⅜ inch thick (about ⅔ cup). Put it into the pie tin or plate and pat it into shape.

Select the flower or flowers you want to use—2 or 3 will probably be enough. Press them upside down (one at a time) into the plaster. Press in firmly to make a deep

impression. Lift the flower away gently. If you are not satisfied with the design, smooth it with your fingers and try again.

Use a pencil or skewer to make 2 holes about 2 inches apart at the top of the plaque while the plaster is still damp. Let the plaque dry thoroughly. When it is dry, remove the plaque, put a piece of yarn, ribbon, or lacing through the holes, knot each end, and hang the plaque up, or wrap it for a gift.

Optional: Write your name and the date on the back of the plaque.

Tissue Paper Flowers

Celebrate springtime with colorful giant flowers!

Materials Needed:

Paper napkins or tissue paper squares (about 12 inches) in assorted colors

Scissors

2 pipe cleaners

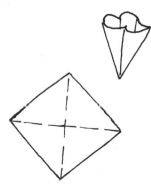

Child's Activity:
Fold the stack in half diagonally 2 times (see illustration). Cut the top edge into 2 scallops. Wrap a pipe cleaner tightly around the bottom inch or so. Unfold and begin carefully separating the layers, fluffing them up toward the center to form the flower. Twist another pipe cleaner onto the first one to make a stem.

Adult's Preparation:
Count out 12 paper napkins or squares of tissue paper (unfold the napkins) and stack them. Help the child with folding and cutting.

Mother's Day

Ribbon-Tied Sachets

Sachets are small pillows of scent to tuck into bureau drawers to make clothes smell nice and fresh. They are very pretty and make thoughtful gifts.

Materials Needed:

Squares of colorful cotton, 1 for each sachet, each 6 inches square ("pink" edges with pinking shears if desired)

Satin or grosgrain ribbon, ¼ inch wide, about 12 inches long for each sachet

Potpourri, 2–4 tablespoons per sachet, store-bought or homemade (see recipe, pp. 61–62. Note: Making potpourri takes about three days)

Artificial flowers (optional)

Adult's Preparation: Assemble materials. Help child tie ribbon if necessary.

Child's Activity: For each sachet, select a piece of fabric and place it facedown on the table. Put a handful of potpourri in the center. Gather up the fabric around the potpourri and tie it securely with a piece of ribbon. Tuck a tiny artificial flower into the bow for decoration, if desired.

Sponge-Painted Flowerpot
A terrific Mother's Day gift!

Materials Needed:
Terra-cotta flowerpot and saucer, small or medium
Small pieces of sponge
Acrylic paints, various colors
Disposable pie tins (one for each color of paint)
Paper towels or newspaper

Adult's Preparation: Prepare work surface and gather materials. Pour a small amount of each paint color to be used into its own pie tin. There should be a piece of sponge for each color paint.

Child's Activity: Dip sponge lightly into paint and blot it once or twice on a paper towel. Lightly dab the sponge on the outside of the flowerpot. Use one color paint or more than one. It's a good idea to let the first color dry a little bit before you start with another color.

If you wish, set a plant in the flowerpot before giving it to Mother.

Painted Pasta Necklace

Pasta shapes can be painted and strung together to make fun "jewelry."

Materials Needed:

Assorted varieties of dried tubular pasta, such as macaroni, rigatoni, macaroni rings, etc.

Narrow cord or string, 28 inches long

Acrylic paints

Paintbrushes

Water

Paper towels

Adult's Preparation: Assemble materials. Cover work area with newspaper. Stiffen one end of string, if desired, by dipping about ½-inch of the string into paint; let dry. Tie a large knot on other end of the string to keep pasta from sliding off. Show child how to paint and string the pasta. Help tie ends of string together to form a necklace when child has finished.

Child's Activity: Paint pasta pieces and let them dry. Slide painted pasta pieces onto string. Tie the ends of the string together to make a necklace.

Memorial Day

A Picnic "Sit-Upon"

A simple little cushion to "sit upon" for picnics and other outings.

Materials Needed:

2 pieces of oilcloth or heavy plastic (like an old table cloth), preferably in bright colors, each 10½ inches × 13 inches

Magazine, 8½ inches × 11 inches

Heavy plastic tape, 2–3 inches wide

Shoelace, 20 inches (optional)

Adult's Preparation: Assemble materials. Help child tape edges and tie handle.

Child's Activity: Place 1 oilcloth square face-down on table. Set magazine in the center. Place second oilcloth square on magazine, right side up. Edges of oilcloth pieces should be even and there should be a border of oilcloth an inch or so all around the magazine. Cut a piece of the heavy tape 13 inches long and place it along the top edge, leaving half its width to fold over to the other side to seal. Tape the remaining three sides.

To make a carrying handle, punch a hole in the top two corners. Tie one end of the shoelace through one hole and the other end through the other hole.

Picnic Mix-Up

This is a fun, nutritious snack to take along on picnics, nature walks, field trips, or vacation trips. The child can concoct her own "recipe" from the ingredients provided.

Materials Needed:
Some or all of the following
   in desired amounts:
   Peanuts
   Raisins
   Sunflower seeds
   Chocolate (or any flavor) morsels
   Dried fruit bits (diced pineapple, apricots, etc.)
   Banana chips
   Flaked coconut
   Jelly bears or other small candies
   O-shaped cereal
   Pretzel sticks
Small scoop (such as a tablespoon or
   ¼-cup measure)
Plastic zip-top quart-size bags or other containers

Adult's Preparation: Assemble materials. Place individual ingredients in different containers and set out on the table.

Child's Activity: Scoop different ingredients into a plastic bag. You may want 1 scoop of some things, 2 or 3 of others. You may even want to leave some things out! When the bag is about half to two-thirds full, close it tightly and shake it to mix everything up. Yummy!

Father's Day

Coin Paperweight

Dads love to receive gifts made especially for them! Or you can make this gift for anyone who has a desk.

Materials Needed:

Block of wood, approximately 3 inches square,
    sanded smooth
5 coins (1 quarter, 2 nickels, 2 pennies,
    for example)
Varnish
Paintbrush
Glue
Pen

Adult's Preparation: Assemble materials. Cover work area with newspapers. Supervise varnishing and gluing. Help child write his name and the date.

Child's Activity: Varnish the wood block. When dry, glue 1 coin on top of the block in the center; glue others, one on each side. Write your name and the date on the bottom of the block.

Manicotti Model Plane

Transform different pasta shapes into a model airplane for a super gift for Dad.

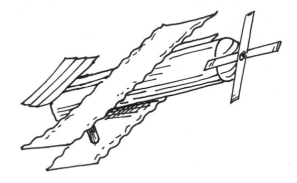

Materials Needed:

1 large manicotti noodle
2 medium rigatoni noodles
2 lasagna noodles
2 fettucini noodles, broken into 2-inch lengths
1 large pasta shell (optional)
Glue

Adult's Preparation: Assemble materials. Help child glue noodles together to form an airplane (see illustration).

Child's Activity: Place 1 lasagna noodle flat on the table. Center manicotti across lasagna noodle and glue. Glue 2 rigatoni noodles upright on the ends of the lasagna noodle. Glue the other lasagna noodle on top of the manicotti; glue to rigatoni noodles, too.

Glue pasta shell to front end of manicotti for a cockpit. Glue 3 fettucini pieces on top of the other end of the manicotti for the tail. Glue 2 fettucini pieces in an X shape and glue it to the front of the "cockpit" shell for a propeller.

Grandparent's Day

Stamp-Stamp Box

Make a little box for Grandmother and Grandfather to keep stamps in. Maybe they will be inspired to write you a letter.

Materials Needed:

Small cardboard box with lid, about 2 inches square
Glue
Enough canceled stamps from old mail to cover the outside of the lid (and the box, optional)
Scissors
Clear varnish or adhesive-backed paper (optional)
Brush for varnish (optional)

Adult's Preparation: Assemble materials. Cover work surface with newspapers.

Child's Activity: Spread a thin layer of glue on the top of the box lid. Stick stamps all over it in a random pattern, covering the top entirely. Any stamps overhanging the edge can be glued down over the lid's sides. Glue more stamps on the lid's sides to cover them completely. Trim the stamps evenly around the bottom edge.

If desired, glue stamps to the box itself, on all four sides. Trim edges evenly at top and bottom.

When glue has set, if you want to, brush or spray top and sides with clear varnish and let dry, or cover with clear adhesive paper.

Greeting Card Picture Frame

The perfect gift for grandparents—a picture of you in a frame you made yourself!

Materials Needed:
Poster board or heavy paper, 8½ inches × 11 inches
Photograph
Glue or tape

Crayons (optional)
Paint (optional)
Stickers (optional)
Ribbon (optional)

Adult's Preparation: Assemble materials. Fold heavy paper in half like a book. On right half of heavy paper, cut out an opening slightly smaller than photograph.

Child's Activity: Decorate the front around the cutout opening any way you like—with crayons, paint, or stickers, for example. Place a photograph inside the "book" so that it shows through the cutout. Glue or tape it in place. Glue ribbon around the cutout opening, if desired. Stand the framed photograph on a table or put it in an envelope and send it to someone special.

Potpourri

Potpourri has been made from summer flowers since the Middle Ages to scent and freshen rooms closed up against the winter's cold. After picking the flowers in summer, children will enjoy watching the changes in them as they dry out. Do the colors change? Do the flowers still have the same smell they did when they were fresh? Potpourri makes an extra-special gift!

Materials Needed:

A collection of flowers, flower petals, and buds that dry well (roses are the traditional base flower for potpourri; carnations, marigolds, zinnias, geraniums, and salvia are also good summer flowers to use)

Large bowl for mixing

Optional:

Aromatic leaves, such as cedar, basil, bay, rose, blackberry, dusty miller, geranium

A few pieces of bark, such as birch or pine

Orange or lemon peel

Cinnamon sticks, cloves, allspice berries, star anise

Adult's Preparation: Help child collect flowers and other ingredients. Be sure to tell the

child not to pick flowers without permission! Also, take care that the child does not collect any samples of poisonous plants.

Spread newspapers on a table indoors (not in direct sunlight) where ingredients can dry undisturbed for several days.

If using citrus peels, trim off the colored part and cut it into strips or slivers.

Child's Activity: Collect some flowers, leaves, and maybe some pretty pieces of bark. Spread them out to dry on newspapers and leave them for several days. When they feel "crispy," they are ready to mix. Put the flowers (whole or in petals), leaves, and bark into a bowl. Add a few cinnamon sticks, cloves, and other whole spices if you wish. Sprinkle in some orange or lemon rind slivers. Place the potpourri in pretty bowls so that you can see and smell a little bit of summer all winter long!

Sand Castle Sculpture

It's fun to make sand castles at the beach in the summertime, but who says you have to go to the beach to make a sand castle? Here is one you can make right at home. Best of all, you won't have to leave it behind for the waves to wash away.

Materials Needed:
Sturdy piece of cardboard for a base, about 8 inches
    × 11 inches or larger
Large paper cup
Small paper cup
Cardboard tube from paper towels
Scissors

Glue (the kind with a brush works best)
Sand, ½ gallon
Large shallow pan or box to put sand in
Tape

Adult's Preparation: Assemble materials. Working on this activity outside would be easiest; if that is not possible, cover work surface with newspapers.

Pour sand into a pan or shallow box, wide enough to roll cups and tubes in.

Child's Activity: If desired, cut small holes in the cups for "windows." Cut the top of the cardboard tube to look like a castle tower (see illustration).

Spread glue over the outside of the cups and the tube. Roll them in the sand until they are completely covered, including the cup bottoms. Let dry.

Turn the cups upside down. Tape the cups and the tube together at the bottom (see illustration), then tape them to the cardboard base.

If desired, spread glue on the top surface of the cardboard base and sprinkle it with sand.

Fourth of July Noisemaker

There'll be a whole lot of shaking going on with this firecracker look-alike!

Materials Needed:

Cardboard tube from bathroom tissue roll

Gift-wrap paper, about 21 inches × 7 inches (preferably in red, white, or blue)

Glue or tape

Scissors

Dried beans or popcorn kernels

Ribbon or yarn, 2 pieces, 8 inches long, 1 piece, 16 inches long (optional)

Adult's Preparation: Assemble materials. Help child cover the tube with paper, tie off, and fringe ends.

Child's Activity: Place paper facedown on table. Center cardboard tube on the bottom edge and roll paper around tube. Secure with glue or tape. Twist one end closed and tie with ribbon or yarn. Put a handful of beans or popcorn kernels into the tube. Twist and tie the remaining end closed. Fringe each end by cutting narrow strips almost up to the tie. Tie a longer piece of ribbon or yarn onto the noisemaker, if desired, to make a handle.

Oompah-pah Pom-poms

Join the parade with your own pom-poms!

Materials Needed:
10–12 plastic shopping bags with cutout handles
String or rubber band
Scissors

Adult's Preparation: Assemble materials. Help child cut bags into strips and tie them together.

Child's Activity: Stack up bags. Trim off bottom edges. Cut bags into strips about 1 inch wide from the bottom up to within about 3 inches from the cutout handles. Separate the strips and fluff them out. Tie string or wrap a rubber band several inches from the top of the bags to hold them together.

Shake out the strips, and you are ready to form a marching band.

Stars and Stripes Collage

You'll want to display our nation's flag on the Fourth of July. Why not one you make yourself?

Materials Needed:
White paper, 8½ inches × 11 inches
Dark blue paper, about 3 inches × 5 inches
Red paper, 8½ inches × 11 inches
Pencil
Glue
Scissors (optional)

Adult's Preparation: Assemble materials. Help child position blue paper and red paper "stripes" to resemble flag.

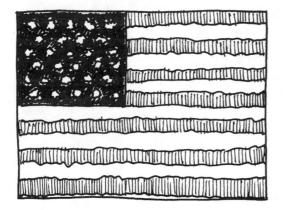

Child's Activity: With the pencil, poke small holes in the blue paper—these will be the "stars" for the flag. (There are fifty stars on a real flag but you don't have to make that many.) Glue the blue paper to the top left corner of the white paper.

Tear or cut the red paper into 11-inch strips, about 1-inch wide. Glue one strip above the bottom edge of the white paper. Glue on another one, leaving about a 1-inch strip of white paper showing between. Repeat until you reach the top of the flag, cutting the last few red strips to fit beside the blue field.

Labor Day

Blue Jean Ginger Boys

Dress up bought cookies in hard-working "clothes" for a treat.

Materials Needed:

Package small gingerbread-boy cookies
Can of vanilla frosting
2–4 tablespoons milk
Blue food coloring
Bowls
Mixing spoons
Small spoon or table knife for spreading (optional)
Red icing gel in tube (optional)
Waxed paper

Adult's Preparation: Assemble materials. Mix frosting in bowl with milk and blue food coloring to get necessary color and consistency.

Child's Activity: Dip gingerbread-boy cookies up to their waists in the blue icing. (Or spread icing on cookies with a small spoon or table knife.) Set on waxed paper to dry.

"Draw" on suspenders and/or bandannas with red icing gel, if desired.

Old-fashioned Rag Ball

Children used to have to make a ball out of rags before rubber was invented. Here's how they did it.

Materials Needed:

Long strips of cloth, about 1–2 inches wide

Adult's Preparation: Assemble materials.

Child's Activity: Make a knot in one end of a strip of cloth and start winding the strip into a ball. Rotate the ball often so it will be as evenly round as possible. Add another strip when the first one runs out by tucking the first inch or so into the wound strips. When the ball is about 4 or 5 inches around, tuck the end of the last strip into the wound ball.

My Favorite T-shirt Pillow

Recycle a favorite T-shirt that has been out-grown but perhaps not "outloved." Maybe you would like to take it to school for rest time.

Materials Needed:

Small T-shirt

Fabric paint in tubes or colored permanent markers
   (optional; T-shirt may already have a design)

Piece of cardboard to fit inside T-shirt
   (if using paint or markers)

Large embroidery needle (with blunt tip)

Thread

Polyester stuffing

Adult's Preparation: Assemble materials. Cover work area with newspapers. Show child how to thread the needle, knot the end of the thread, and do a simple whipstitch.

(You may have to do the sewing for younger children.)

Child's Activity: If using paints or markers, slip cardboard inside the T-shirt to keep colors from bleeding through to the other side. Decorate the T-shirt as you wish with fabric paint or markers. When dry, remove the cardboard. Sew the neck and arm openings closed. Fill shirt with stuffing until it is nice and plump. Sew the bottom edge closed. Is it time for a nap?

"Hand-y" Crayon Cup

Keep your new school crayons handy in this container. Don't forget to practice writing letters and numbers.

Materials Needed:

Clean soup or other can with top removed and
    inside edges smoothed
Wallpaper or construction paper about 8 inches $\times$
    16 inches
Scissors
Acrylic paint
Brush
Small paintbrush (optional)
Glue
Rubber bands (optional)

Adult's Preparation: Assemble materials. Cover work area with newspapers. Trim wallpaper to fit around can with an overlap of about an inch. Top and bottom edges should be trimmed to fit just inside the rim of the can.

Child's Activity: Brush the palm and fingers of one of your hands with paint. Press your painted hand onto the center of the paper and lift it away carefully. You might want to paint on the year underneath your handprint with a small brush. Clean your hand and the brush. Let the handprint and date dry.

Fit the handprinted paper around the can, overlapping the ends. Glue the end generously and hold it firmly until it stays glued down. You could secure it with a couple of rubber bands until the glue sets.

Columbus Day

A Compass for Columbus

To "sail the ocean blue," Christopher Columbus needed a compass to make sure he was going in the right direction. Here's a version you can make.

Materials Needed:

Paper plate, 6 inches

Brass paper fastener

Construction paper, 1 sheet any color

Crayons

Scissors

Glue (optional)

Adult's Preparation: Assemble materials. Explain to your child that a real compass points to magnetic north.

Child's Activity: Cut out a 4–5-inch-long pointer or arrow from construction paper. Make a small hole in the center of the pointer. Make another small hole in the center of the paper plate. Attach the pointer to the front of the paper plate with a brass paper fastener; spread the fastener's "wings" flat on the back of the paper plate.

With crayons, write *N*, *S*, *E*, and *W* on the front of the plate (see illustration). Decorate

the compass with cutouts or drawings of the sun, moon, and stars if desired.

Glow-in-the-Dark Star Chart

Columbus and other early sailors used the stars to navigate, as well as compasses and other instruments.

Materials Needed:

Dark blue or black poster board, 16 inches × 20 inches

Adhesive-backed glow-in-the-dark paper in a bright color, 1 sheet

Scissors

Adult's Preparation: Assemble materials. Cut out crescent moon and some large and small star shapes. Be prepared to give child a simple explanation of phases of the moon and constellations.

Child's Activity: Arrange stars on the dark poster board to form a picture of "the Big Dipper"; add crescent moon (see illustration). Hang the chart in your bedroom so you can see the stars glow in the dark.

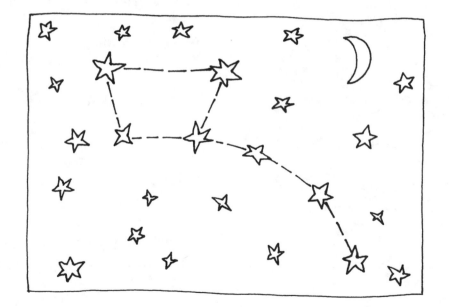

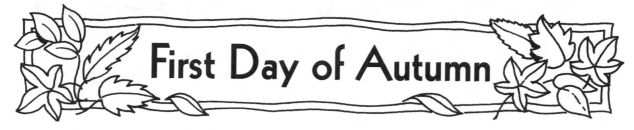

First Day of Autumn

Autumn Leaf Rubbings

After taking a walk to collect pretty leaves, make leaf rubbings with some of them.

Materials Needed:

Drawing paper, such as newsprint, 8½ inches × 11 inches or larger

Crayons or chalk

Glue and tape

Leaves (still pliable, not dry)

Adult's Preparation: Assemble materials. Help child position leaves on paper and show child how to rub crayon or chalk over the paper to capture the leaf's design.

Child's Activity: Arrange leaf or leaves face-down on paper. Glue them in place. Cover with another piece of paper. Tape edges so the paper won't move around. Choose a crayon or piece of chalk and rub it lightly back and forth across the top paper until the pattern of the leaf shows through.

Fall-Is-in-the-Air Pomander

Bring the scents of autumn inside with this ball of spices.

Materials Needed:

Plastic foam ball, about 2—4 inches in diameter
Glue (the kind with a brush works best)
Mixed chopped pickling spices, about ½ cup
Shallow pan or box to put spices in
Ribbon, 16 inches long

Adult's Preparation: Assemble materials. Cover work surface with newspapers. Spread pickling spices in a shallow pan or box. Help child cover ball with glue and spices and help tie ribbon around the finished pomander.

Child's Activity: Spread glue on half the foam ball; roll the glued half in the pan or box of spices until it is thickly covered. Press the spices down into the glue so they will stay on. Let glue dry. Repeat with other half of the ball. Tie a ribbon around the ball, leaving ends long enough to make a loop to hang the ball. Put a little glue on ribbon to secure it if necessary. You might put it on your bedroom door.

Spooky Spider

A little bit spooky but a whole lot of fun for Halloween!

Materials Needed:

Construction paper, black and yellow (1 sheet of
black and small piece of yellow for each spider)
Glue
Rubber band or string
Stapler and staples

Adult's Preparation: Assemble materials. Cut black construction paper into one 4-inch circle for the body and 8 leg strips (¾ inch × 11 inches. Cut out small yellow circles for eyes.

Child's Activity: Fold the strips into accordion pleats and glue them to the black circle, 4 on each side (see illustration). Glue yellow circles to the top of the black circle for eyes. Staple a rubber band or string to the center of the top side of the black circle. Hang the "spooky spider" up for a Halloween decoration.

Ghost

This little ghost seems to fly through the air when hung in a breezy spot.

Materials Needed:

3 square white paper napkins
Black or orange yarn, 8 inches for each ghost
Black marker

Adult's Preparation: Assemble materials. Help child tie the yarn to form ghost's head.

Child's Activity: Unfold 2 of the napkins and spread them flat, one on top of the other. Unfold the remaining napkin and crush it into a ball. Place the ball in the center of the flat napkins. Gather the napkins around the ball and tie snugly with a piece of yarn. Turn upside down and draw some eyes and a mouth on the ghost's head.

Thanksgiving

Birdie Buffet

Watch the birds flock to this easy-to-make feeding station!

Materials Needed:

Large pine cone
Heavy twine or wire, 12 inches long
½ cup peanut butter
½ cup shortening or lard
½ cup birdseed mixture
Large bowl
Mixing spoon
Small spoon or table knife for spreading
Pie tin

Adult's Preparation: Assemble materials. Tie twine or wire to pine cone for a hanging loop.

Child's Activity: Mix peanut butter and shortening together. Spread this on the pine cone and stuff it down into the spaces between the "petals."

Pour birdseed mixture into the pie tin. Roll the pine cone in the birdseed, pressing the seeds into the peanut butter. Press more seeds in by hand to cover the pine cone thickly.

Hang the pine cone feeder in a tree. How

many different kinds of birds come to visit their "birdie buffet"?

Pine Cone Turkey

Use these for place cards or a centerpiece on the Thanksgiving table.

Materials Needed:

Large pine cone, 1 for each turkey

Construction paper, red and orange (1 sheet of each color)

Scissors

Glue

Black pen or crayon

Adult's Preparation: Assemble materials. Make a pattern for the turkey's head and feet (see illustration).

Child's Activity: Trace your hand on the red paper and the orange paper. Cut these out and put them together so that both the red and the orange fingers show. Glue them together. Stick the red and orange "tail feathers" in place on the back of the upright cone. Glue if necessary. Cut the head of the turkey

from red construction paper. Draw a face on it. Glue the head onto the front of the pine cone. Cut out some orange turkey feet and glue them to the bottom of the cone.

Pilgrim Hat Place Mats

At the first Thanksgiving, Native Americans invited the Pilgrims to a feast to celebrate the good harvest. Make some place mats to look like the Pilgrims' hats for your Thanksgiving table.

Materials Needed:

Construction paper, black, white, and gray (1 sheet each of black and gray, and piece of white for each hat)
Scissors
Glue

Adult's Preparation: Assemble materials. Sketch outline of Pilgrim hat on black paper (see illustration). Help child cut out hat.

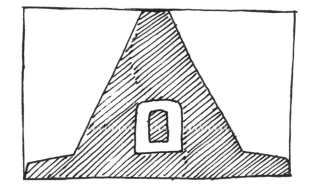

Child's Activity: Cut out shape of Pilgrim hat from black construction paper. Glue hat shape onto piece of gray construction paper. Cut a "buckle" out of white paper and glue it onto the hat (see illustration).

First Day of Winter

Swingin' Snowman Mobile

This jolly snowman will swing and sway through those frosty days of winter.

Materials Needed:

Construction paper, white and black (1 sheet of white and piece of black for each snowman)
Construction paper, other colors (optional)
Glue
Crayons (optional)
Thin yarn, crochet thread, or string, 28 inches long
Glitter (optional)

Adult's Preparation: Assemble materials.

Trace circles onto white paper and hat shape onto black paper for child to cut out. Help tie pieces together.

Child's Activity: Cut 3 circles (about 4 inches, 6 inches, and 8 inches in diameter) from white construction paper. Cut out a top hat shape from the black construction paper and glue to top of smallest white circle. Cut out smaller shapes for eyes, buttons, and any other features you want to add to your snowman. Glue them on the circles. (These can be drawn with crayons instead.)

Punch holes in the top and bottom of each

edge all the way across; slip dowel into pocket. Tie yarn onto dowel ends to finish wall hanging. Remind child to glue a flame on top of a candle each day of Hanukkah.

Child's Activity: Cut out menorah shape from felt. Glue onto background piece of felt. Cut candles from felt and glue onto background above menorah. Cut out 9 flame shapes from yellow or red felt. Glue a flame on center candle right away. Then glue a flame on top of 1 of the 8 candles left each day of Hanukkah until all of the 9 candles have been "lit."

Gold Coin Pouch

Make a little pouch to carry your Hanukkah coins in.

Materials Needed:

Circle of felt, any color (about 8 inches in diameter)
Scissors
Ribbon, thick yarn, or shoelace, 32 inches long

Adult's Preparation: Assemble materials. Help cut slits in felt. Help thread ribbon through laces.

Child's Activity: Cut ½-inch slits every inch or so about 1 inch from the outer edge of the felt (see illustration).

    Weave the ribbon, yarn, or shoelace through the slits. Tie the ends into a knot.

Gather the felt along the ribbon into a pouch. Put coins into the pouch for safekeeping.

doily, if desired. Help child assemble and decorate house.

Child's Activity: Generously spread the bottom edge and two side edges of 4 graham cracker squares with frosting. Set the cracker squares upright on the cardboard to form the four walls of the cottage. Don't worry about any icing that "oozes" out of the edges—it will look like snow!

Spread frosting on all three edges of the two triangular pieces of graham crackers; place them upright on two opposite walls. Place 2 remaining square crackers on top for a roof, using more icing as needed for "glue."

If desired, put shredded wheat biscuits on the roof with frosting to simulate a thatched roof. Decorate the remainder of the house with assorted candies using frosting as "glue" to hold them in place.

Gumdrop Tree

A colorful, sparkly, tasty centerpiece!

Materials Needed:

Small flowerpot
Gravel or block of plastic foam (to anchor branch)
Small tree branch
Bag multicolored gumdrops

Adult's Preparation: Assemble materials. The branch should have plenty of little twigs to stick the gumdrops on!

Child's Activity: Center the tree branch in the flowerpot and surround it with gravel to hold it upright. If you prefer, put a block of plastic foam into the flowerpot and anchor the branch in it.

Stick gumdrops on the ends of the twigs of the branch.

Birthday

Happy Birthday Crown

The birthday child is king or queen for the day!

Materials Needed:

Construction paper, any color for base of crown (2 sheets), other colors as desired for decorating

Scissors

Tape or stapler and staples

Glue

Crayons

Glitter

Adult's Preparation: Assemble materials. Cut paper into a strip 6 inches wide by about 22 inches long (tape several strips together if necessary). Pencil a line lengthwise across

the strip 3 inches from the bottom. Starting 2 inches from one end, draw triangles above the pencil line to make points; leave 2 inches at the other end for overlapping the ends to form into a ring. (See illustration.) Write *Happy Birthday* across the bottom of the crown if desired. Assist child with cutting if necessary.

Child's Activity: Cut out points on top of the crown. Decorate the crown as desired with construction-paper "jewel" cutouts, crayons, and/or glitter. Put the ends of the crown together and tape or staple closed. Happy Birthday!

My Book About Me

All children want to know more about themselves. A birthday is a good time to make their very own book.

Materials Needed:
Construction paper, any color
  (3 or more sheets)
Stapler and staples
Crayons

Adult's Preparation: Assemble materials. Help child write as needed.

Child's Activity: Stack 3 or more sheets of paper, fold in half like a book, and staple folded side to hold the book together.

Draw and color pictures on each page.

Here are some suggested topics and illustrations. Do one per page. Add more as desired.

My name is _____. (Draw a picture of yourself)

This is my family:
   (Draw members of your family; don't forget pets!)

I am ___ years old.
   (Draw a cake with that many candles on it.)

I live at _____. (Write your
   address; draw a picture of your house.)

My telephone number is _____.
   (Draw a picture of a telephone.)

My favorite toy is _____. (Draw the toy.)

Notes for Your Own Craft Ideas